Books are to be returned on or before
the last date

KT-558-190

War

Geoff Barker

Evans

TITLES IN THE VOICES SERIES:

AIDS • CHILD LABOUR • DRUGS ON THE STREET • GANGS

HUNGER • POVERTY • RACE HATE • RELIGIOUS EXTREMISM

VIOLENCE • VIOLENCE ON THE SCREEN • WAR

Published by Evans Brothers Limited
2A Portman Mansions
Chiltern Street
London W1U 6NR

First published 2009
© copyright Evans Brothers 2009

VISIT OUR WEBSITE
Evans
www.evansbooks.co.uk

Produced for Evans Brothers Limited by
Monkey Puzzle Media Ltd
Little Manor Farm, The Street
Brundish, Woodbridge
Suffolk IP13 8BL, UK

British Library Cataloguing in Publication Data
Barker, Geoff
War. – (Voices)
1. War – Juvenile literature
I. Title
303.6'6

ISBN-13: 978 0 237 53722 7

Editor: Susie Brooks
Designer: Mayer Media Ltd
Picture research: Susie Brooks and Lynda Lines
Graphs and charts: Martin Darlison, Encompass Graphics

Picture acknowledgements
Photographs were kindly supplied by the following: Alamy 18 (Jack Picone); Corbis 1 (Doug Niven/epa), 6 (Lynsey Addario), 7 (Antoine Gyori), 11 (Reuters), 13 (WEDA), 25 (Reuters), 39 (Doug Niven/epa), 40 (Oliver Coret/In Visu); Getty Images front cover (AFP), 8 (Popperfoto), 10, 14, 16 (AFP), 22, 27, 28 (Hulton Archive), 30, 32 (AFP), 34 (Hulton Archive), 38, 42–43 (AFP); Human Rights Watch 21; PA Photos 20 (AP), 33 (Aaron Favila/AP), 37 (Hidajet Delic/AP); Panos Pictures 17 (Frederik Naumann), 19 (Jeroen Oerlemans), 35 (Alfredo Caliz), 41 (David Rose); Photoshot 36 (Eye Ubiquitous); Rex Features 26, 29 (Sipa), 45.

Cover picture: A US Army soldier passes an Iraqi woman while on patrol in the Al-Dora neighbourhood of Baghdad, Iraq, in July 2008.

CONTENTS

WHAT IS WAR?

War is armed, violent fighting, usually between two or more countries or groups. Some wars spring from conflict over resources; others involve clashes between people with different beliefs. Disputes like this happen all around the world.

Sudanese refugees wait for food and assistance in February 2008, after their village in western Darfur was bombed by government forces.

Danger for all

Wars are generally fought between armed forces. But in wartime, you do not have to be a soldier to be in danger – sometimes civilians are attacked too. When war broke out in the Darfur region of western Sudan in 2003, many people were forced to flee their homes. Mohammed, 20, is one of up to 250,000 Darfurian refugees who crossed the border to safety in neighbouring Chad:

❝ Government forces attacked our village with vehicles, helicopters and missiles. They killed many of us. The rest of us fled and got lost in the desert. We brought nothing with us. Now we are here [in a refugee camp]... But we bring food shortages and security problems... so local people [in Chad] are not very happy to have us here. We will stay here until we can move to a safer camp. ❞

Injury and death

During wars, ordinary people suddenly have to cope with death and terrible injuries. Often they cannot get access to the care that they need. In 1991, Iraq suffered many casualties in the bombardments of the First Gulf War. Medical resources were stretched, and hospital conditions poor. This unnamed Iraqi surgeon worked 20-hour shifts in a Baghdad hospital, helping injured people without anaesthetics:

❝ I have no clean water to wash [my hands], no alcohol to kill germs... I move hour after hour from the open wounds of one person to another, spreading infection. I cannot help my patients. ❞

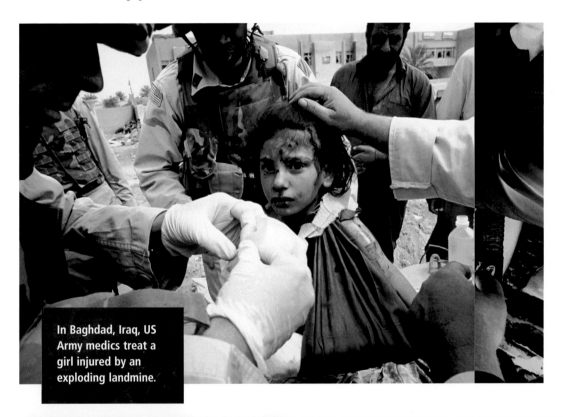

In Baghdad, Iraq, US Army medics treat a girl injured by an exploding landmine.

FIRST GULF WAR

Western forces invaded Iraq in 1991 to end hostilities with Kuwait. The war involved:

- **110,000 aerial attacks in 42 days**
- **1 attack every 30 seconds**
- **88,500 tonnes of bombs**
- **200,000 Iraqi deaths**
- **148 US casualties.**

"I have seen war. I have seen war on land and sea. I have seen blood running from the wounded. I have seen the dead in the mud. I have seen cities destroyed. I have seen children starving. I have seen the agony of mothers and wives. I hate war."

Franklin D Roosevelt, 32nd US President (1933–1945).

HAS WARFARE ALWAYS BEEN THE SAME?

People have fought and waged war with each other since the beginning of history. In some ways, wars are the same now as ever before: soldiers die, and the side with the most powerful forces wins. But have the basic targets of warfare changed over time?

A soldier's war

World War I (1914–1918) was meant to be 'the war to end all wars', a final conflict to decide which nations were the most powerful. Partly as a result, almost 10 million soldiers died in the fighting. Those arriving at the front line were mostly ordinary young men who had only just left school. Charles Alexander, an 18-year-old from Oxford, England, was among the millions who were called up to fight:

❝ This is a million miles away from home, but I can dream of summers in the garden can't I? The trenches are foul. There are the rats, the lice... and if the weather's bad, and it rains for days, standing in the water can rot your foot away. But I'm still alive, thank God. Hundreds died when the shelling began again yesterday... my best friend Jimmy died in my arms, his blood all over me... ❞

During World War I, troops on both sides fought from long, narrow trenches dug into the ground. These British soldiers are defending their positions on the Western Front in France, 1917.

Civilian murder

In many more recent conflicts, enemy forces have deliberately targeted non-soldiers, or civilians, during the fighting. When war struck the African country of Rwanda in 1994, forces of the Hutu tribe deliberately killed more than 800,000 people from the rival Tutsi tribe. Stephanie Nyombayire, aged 8, was staying in Congo when her family became innocent victims of the Hutu soldiers:

❝ The first day, my grandmother was shot in front of her 15–year–old daughter, my aunt. My grandfather was killed the next day. Those who were lucky enough could pay to be shot rather than face the machetes, clubs and whatever else they could find... ❞

"[The main victims] were the Tutsi people of Rwanda, three-quarters of whom were completely eradicated for the simple crime of being Tutsi – for who they were, not for anything they might have done."
KY Amoako, Executive Secretary of the United Nations Economic Commission for Africa, 2003.

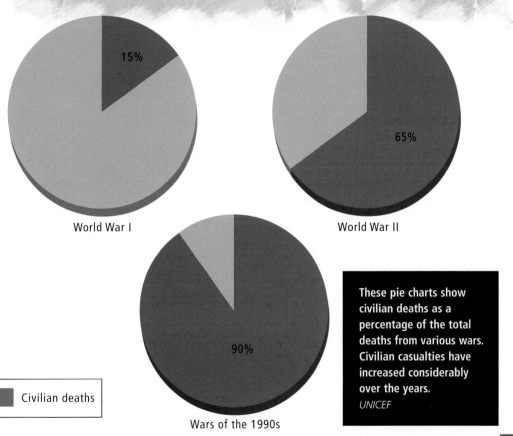

15%

World War I

65%

World War II

90%

Wars of the 1990s

Civilian deaths

These pie charts show civilian deaths as a percentage of the total deaths from various wars. Civilian casualties have increased considerably over the years.
UNICEF

WHY START A WAR?

People have many different reasons for beginning a war. They may be fighting to gain power of a country or ownership of land. Sometimes resources, such as oil, are at stake. At other times war is an attempt to put an end to other aggressions.

War on terror

In 2001, the USA invaded Afghanistan. This was in response to the al-Qaeda terrorist attacks of 9/11, which targeted New York and Washington, DC and killed nearly 3,000 civilians. Afghanistan provided a safe haven for al-Qaeda and its leader, Osama bin Laden. Many people felt the invasion was a necessary step in fighting terror around the world. Mark, an American, explains:

❝ I think Afghanistan was definitely the correct thing to do. There were terrorist training camps there. And bin Laden used to hang out in Afghanistan. And the Taliban who were in power at the time supported al-Qaeda. So after 9/11, we had to let the world know that we aren't going to just sit by and let someone kill our citizens like that. ❞

In November 2001, troops from the Afghan Northern Alliance celebrate the capture of the city of Kabul from the ruling Taliban.

WAR LAW

According to international law, a country may use force against another in two cases:

● In self-defence – to protect itself from an aggressor.

● To protect global peace and security.

UN charter, Chapter VII, articles 42 and 51

Civil disputes

Many political and religious or ethnic disputes result in civil war, between rival groups within one country. In 1980, the Peruvian government came under attack from a rebel group called Shining Path, who wanted to change the way the country was run. Years of fighting followed, including a bloody massacre in Lucanamarca in 1983. Juan Carlos was only 17 at the time:

“ Shining Path came for revenge. Many people in our village used to support these cowards. It was awful... They poured boiling water over us and hacked at us with machetes and axes... My wife was with child and they killed her. Women, children, even a baby... none of us will ever forget what we saw on that bloody day. ”

Shining Path believed that vicious attacks like this would make the country's leaders take notice of their cause.

Relatives of some of Shining Path's victims weep in memory of their loved-ones at a march in Ayacucho, Peru.

"In that case [Lucanamarca], the principal thing is that we dealt them [the government] a devastating blow... they understood that they were dealing with a different kind of people's fighters, that we weren't the same as those they had fought before."

Abimael Guzmán, founder and leader of Shining Path.

WHY BECOME A SOLDIER?

Every soldier risks death or injury when he or she goes into battle. Soldiers may also have to kill others – people they have never met and who have done them no harm. So why do people choose to become soldiers?

Defending the country

Many young people join the armed forces with a view to defending their country. Otto Meier, aged 18, has recently joined the German army and enjoys his job. He believes that it is right to be a soldier and is happy to protect his family, friends and country in any conflict:

❝ My job is to kill other humans, if need be. But other professional soldiers have trained to kill me, in the same way I have trained to kill them. I'm willing to kill and to die, because I am safeguarding the lives of my loved ones, and everyone else in this country. ❞

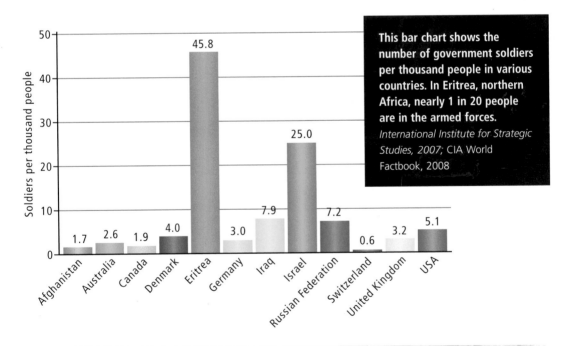

This bar chart shows the number of government soldiers per thousand people in various countries. In Eritrea, northern Africa, nearly 1 in 20 people are in the armed forces.
International Institute for Strategic Studies, 2007; CIA World Factbook, 2008

Soldiers per thousand people:
- Afghanistan 1.7
- Australia 2.6
- Canada 1.9
- Denmark 4.0
- Eritrea 45.8
- Germany 3.0
- Iraq 7.9
- Israel 25.0
- Russian Federation 7.2
- Switzerland 0.6
- United Kingdom 3.2
- USA 5.1

"Being a soldier is about trust, teamwork, mutual respect, leadership, professionalism, discipline and honour. Soldiers don't just prepare for war; they help local communities, assist in peacekeeping duties and provide humanitarian aid, at home and overseas."
New Zealand Army recruitment page, 2008.

"I hate war as only a soldier who has lived it can, only as one who has seen its brutality, its futility [uselessness], its stupidity."

General Dwight D Eisenhower, former Supreme Commander of the Allied Forces, World War II.

An Australian soldier stands guard in front of a burning house during conflict in Dili, East Timor in 2006.

False expectations

Other people are attracted by the physical challenge of being a soldier. But some recruits discover too late that the reality of war is very different from their everyday training. They may struggle to cope with the fighting, or find themselves doubting the cause. Bryan Henderson is a former officer in the Australian army who served in East Timor in 2001. He now feels that being a soldier does not achieve anything good:

❝ You know, being a soldier is a dirty and ugly job. You will kill people, or help others to kill people. Kill a hundred, kill just one person and you'll have made the world an uglier place. In the end, it's just wrong. It was certainly the wrong profession for me. It doesn't make much difference if it seemed like a just cause at first. ❞

CAN WAR BE JUSTIFIED?

Country leaders sometimes feel that they can justify an invasion or war. For example, civilians in a country may be suffering from abuse and harm by their leaders. Is it right to think that a war to help those people is fair?

Ending cruelty

When Saddam Hussein ruled Iraq, many Iraqis were beaten, tortured and killed by the police or army. Most were ethnic Kurds or Shi'ite Muslims, who Saddam saw as a threat to his Arab, Sunni Muslim regime. Muneer Ahmed, aged 19, survived a savage attack:

❝ Women and children were... blindfolded. Some were dragged off to torture chambers, their nails ripped out, ears sliced off... I was beaten with pipes, whatever they could lay their hands on. I blacked out. I'd been dragged to a mass grave, and woke with corpses all around me. ❞

Some people felt that it was right for other countries to invade Iraq in 2003, if it stopped ordinary Iraqi people from being treated in this way.

In 2003, a huge mass grave with over 2,000 bodies was discovered at Hillah in Iraq. These were just some of the victims of atrocities during Saddam's regime.

"We have a moral obligation to intervene where evil is in control. Today, that place is Iraq."
Elie Wiesel, World War II Holocaust survivor and Nobel Peace Prize winner, 2003.

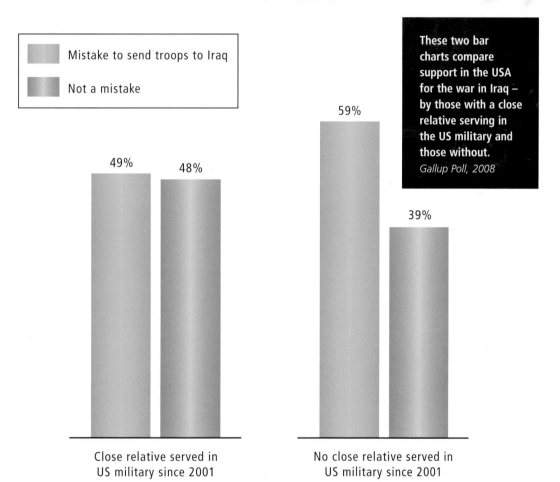

Mistake to send troops to Iraq

Not a mistake

These two bar charts compare support in the USA for the war in Iraq – by those with a close relative serving in the US military and those without.
Gallup Poll, 2008

49%   48%

59%

39%

Close relative served in
US military since 2001

No close relative served in
US military since 2001

Making matters worse

Other people feel that going to war is not the answer, and can even make matters worse. Yusuf Shammari is a Sunni Muslim. He was living in Baghdad with two young children, Mahmoud and Samah, when his wife died in a bomb attack. Yusuf blames the 2003 invasion for the current chaos in Iraq:

❝ Iraq is in a mess... just look it at. This is civil war now. No one in their right mind could say that the Americans and British got it right [with the invasion of Iraq in 2003]. Yes, we had Saddam... and he did awful things to some Shi'ites and Kurds. But people knew who to trust and who to steer clear of. When I was a kid, we all used to play together. I feel sorry for my children growing up in Iraq. ❞

SHOULD YOU FIGHT FOR YOUR COUNTRY?

Many people love their country and are proud to be citizens. But does loving your country mean you should be ready to fight, and perhaps die, for it?

Dying for a cause

Some people are willing to kill or die for a cause they truly believe in. For example, Israelis and Palestinians have been fighting for decades over land that both groups feel is their own. In 2008, Israel attacked the Gaza strip, Palestinian territory. Over a thousand Palestinians died as a result. Such events have made some young Palestinians willing to die for their country:

❝ I want to be a martyr... I hope when I am older to blow myself up. My father was killed in Gaza. He was happy to be a martyr. I would rather die too... than see the people who killed my father living here. I think it is my destiny to die here too. ❞

A young Palestinian throws a petrol bomb at an Israeli army vehicle in August 2007.

> "There is no flag large enough to cover the shame of killing innocent people for a purpose which is unattainable."
> Howard Zinn, US historian and anti-war lobbyist, 1993.

Anti-war demonstrators in Lisbon, Portugal hold up a white dove symbol of peace.

Living for peace

Many people feel loyal to their country but would not go as far as to fight for it. Stefan Kieslowski, a 16-year-old from Poland, is a pacifist – he would not take part in any kind of war. He loves Poland, but does not think it should ever be defended using violence:

❝ I'm patriotic. I'm Polish and I'm proud of that... but I wouldn't fight for my country. We have laws to stop us killing innocent people – it's totally wrong. So how come it is OK to kill someone during war? The enemy is made up of people just like you and me. Even if someone was pointing a gun at me I don't know if I'd be able to kill them. I just hope I'm never in that position. ❞

CAN NORMAL LIFE CARRY ON DURING A WAR?

When a country goes to war, life is often turned upside down. People may be unable to go to work or school, and services such as transport and power supplies suffer. Is it ever possible for normal life to carry on in the midst of the fighting?

Disruption and fear

For many civilians in war-torn countries, daily life is filled with fear. They face not only the risk of attack, but also the threat of hunger and disease as access to food, water and medical care is disrupted. Some may be forced into hiding, with little means to survive. Eduardo suffered years of hardship in Angola, Africa in the 1990s:

❝ Most of my life I couldn't go to school at all because of the war here in Angola. Before we moved to this village I lived in the forest with my family. For two years we were always running and trying to escape from soldiers chasing us. One time we hid in the river to escape. We didn't have any food, shelter, tents – nothing. ❞

Women and children take refuge in a bombed-out building in the war-torn town of Kuito, Angola in 1993.

"There are wounded who do not get sufficient treatment, there are people who do not have safe drinking water, there are, first and foremost, tens of thousands of people who are now being besieged or in areas of crossfire."

Jan Egeland, UN relief coordinator in Beirut, Lebanon, 2006.

A Lebanese boy rescues some books from what remains of his home in Tyre, after a bombing raid in 2006.

Life goes on

Sometimes during wars it is possible for a few normal activities to continue. Sanaa Mehanna, 11, lives in Beirut, Lebanon. She stayed there through the 34-day war between Lebanon and Israel, which finished in August 2006. Sanaa explains how life was restricted during the war, but she was still able to do some normal things:

LEBANESE CASUALTIES

Estimate of casualties during the 2006 Lebanon War:

Civilians: 1,200 dead; 5,100 wounded

Military: 500 dead; 500 wounded

Lebanon is thought to have suffered ten casualties to every Israeli casualty.

❝ Some schools got destroyed in the bombing, but we were lucky. During the war, no one wanted to go out... the streets were empty. It was scary when the bombs went off... but most of the time we just watched the news on the television. I still saw my friends and we did play sometimes. ❞

CAN WAR BRING OUT THE BEST IN PEOPLE?

Wartime experiences can be the most difficult times that anyone has to live through. Do these hard times force people to work together and help each other, or do they bring out the worst in people?

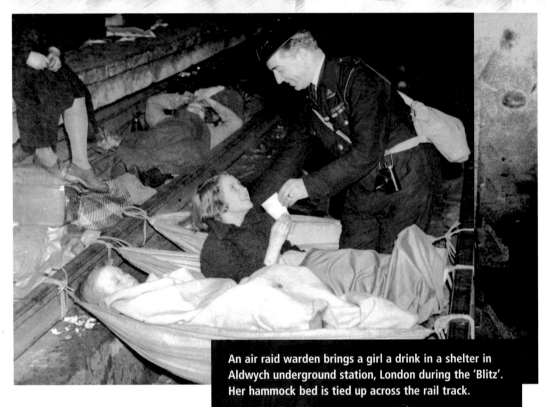

An air raid warden brings a girl a drink in a shelter in Aldwych underground station, London during the 'Blitz'. Her hammock bed is tied up across the rail track.

Helping others

During World War II, a 'Blitz' of German bombs rained down on London and other big cities and ports. Facing the bombs side by side gave many British people a sense of togetherness that became known as the 'Blitz spirit'. Minnie Bell felt the experience brought out the best in people:

❝ The Blitz went on for nearly nine months, but we all just got on with it, didn't we? We came out of our shelter one day and our house had been bombed. Neighbours from across the road saw us looking a bit shell shocked I suppose, and just came up to us and said, 'You can stay with us if you like.' ❞

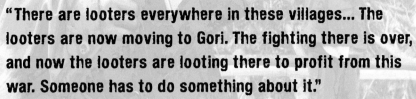

"There are looters everywhere in these villages... The looters are now moving to Gori. The fighting there is over, and now the looters are looting there to profit from this war. Someone has to do something about it."

An army officer in the disputed region of South Ossetia, Georgia, August 2008.

Reacting badly

The fear, anger and confusion brought by war can also have a negative effect on civilian behaviour. Conflict is often accompanied by crimes such as vandalism and theft. When troops withdrew from the Georgian city of Gori after fighting in 2008, chaos filled the streets. Looters plundered goods from shops, while others felt ashamed as they turned a blind eye. This local man did not wish to be identified:

❝ The looting started nearly as soon as the soldiers left... I live next to the shop and heard the sound of the door getting kicked in. These people [the shopkeepers] are my friends but I didn't want to confront the... [looters]. It's too dangerous. I hid upstairs until it went quiet again... There's no excuse. People just act in a shameful way. ❞

Armed looters take household items from a village near Gori, Georgia, in 2008.

IS IT RIGHT FOR WOMEN TO FIGHT?

History is peppered with stories about women in battle, such as the fierce Amazonians from South America. But many societies have banned women from military service. Should women be allowed to fight in wars?

An equal struggle

Many people feel that men and women should be allowed to do the same jobs, including joining the army and fighting for their country. It is not always easy for women to be accepted as soldiers, but often this makes them more determined. Sally Gummerson fought for the British Army in Afghanistan in 2001:

❝ As a female soldier, it is sometimes hard to be treated as an equal. I think it confuses a lot of people that I want to do this job. I love this job. War is seen by most as a male activity. You have to be tough to do this job, but you don't have to be a man to do it. ❞

Female recruits for the US Marine Corps begin their rigorous training at a 'boot camp' in Parris Island, South Carolina.

"In order to defend our values and freedoms, our armed forces must reflect them as well. Equality of opportunity is a fundamental part of those values."
Paul Keetch, UK Liberal Democrat spokesman for defence, 2002.

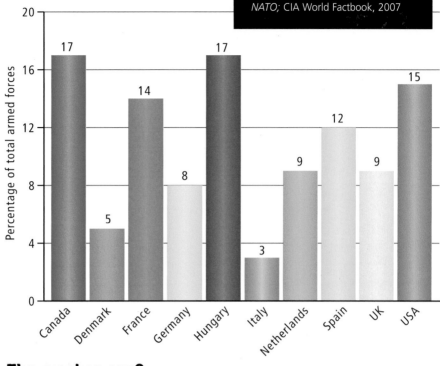

This bar chart shows the percentage of armed forces who are women, in various countries.
NATO; CIA World Factbook, 2007

Percentage of total armed forces

20 — 16 — 12 — 8 — 4 — 0

Canada 17 | Denmark 5 | France 14 | Germany 8 | Hungary 17 | Italy 3 | Netherlands 9 | Spain 12 | UK 9 | USA 15

The weaker sex?

Some people argue that warfare is not a traditional woman's role – for a reason. They point out that most women are physically weaker than men, so it is not realistic to expect women to be as good at fighting. As one male writer on an Internet forum said:

❝ This is about killing other men with superior force, not playing up to people's feelings of gender equality. When it comes down to it, if you can carry the same load as me, kill a strong man with your hands when he attacks you or me, and carry me home when I fall, you are welcome to fight alongside me no matter what sex you are. Reality is, how many women can honestly lay claim to these things? ❞

ISLAMIC FEMALE SOLDIERS

Libya is the only Islamic nation to have women in the military. Colonel Qadaffi employs a 200-strong unit of female personal bodyguards. They make up about 0.2% of an estimated total of 100,000 Libyan soldiers.

WHY ARE THERE CHILD SOLDIERS?

There may be as many as half a million child soldiers worldwide. They serve as spies, messengers, porters and sentries, as well as battling on the front line. How is it that children end up fighting adults' wars?

A glamorous game?

Some children actually want to fight or are attracted to the glamour of becoming a soldier. They may look forward to the power and excitement of using weapons such as guns and machetes. In 2004, 12-year-old Nijad joined a rebel army in Iraq:

❝ I joined the Mahdi army to fight the Americans. Last night I fired a rocket-propelled grenade against a tank. ❞

Other children become soldiers in the hope that it will somehow improve their lives. A 17-year-old girl from the Revolutionary Armed Forces of Colombia explains:

❝ I joined the guerrilla to escape... I thought I'd get some money and could be independent. ❞

"Many [children] choose to join an armed group because they feel safer under its protection. Most have little concept of what life as a [soldier] entails until it is too late to back out. In exchange for comradeship, food, and protection, children are exposed to disease, physical exhaustion, injury, sudden death, and torture at the hands of the enemy."

Sebastian Brett, Human Rights Watch report on Colombian child soldiers, 2003.

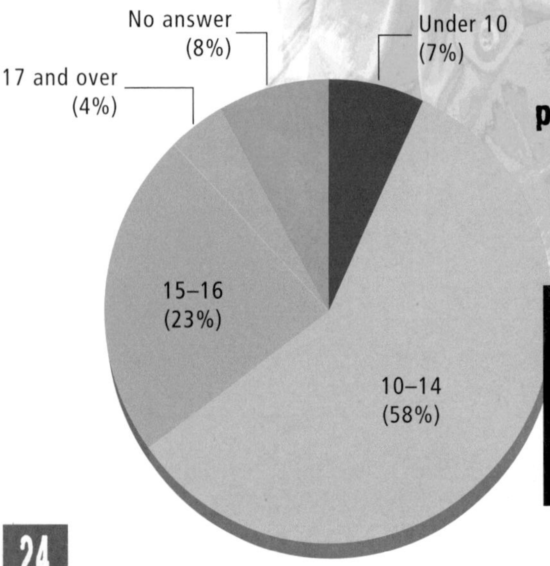

No answer (8%)

17 and over (4%)

Under 10 (7%)

15–16 (23%)

10–14 (58%)

This pie chart shows the age at entry into the armed forces, among a sample of child soldiers in Colombia. More than one in ten of these children admitted that their entry was forced.
Human Rights Watch, 2002

A 12-year-old soldier in Myanmar (Burma) raises his gun. He fights for the Karen rebel army against the military government of his country, which also uses thousands of child soldiers.

Forced to fight

Mostly, children do not choose to join an army – they are forced. In Uganda, Africa, for example, the Lord's Resistance Army (LRA) actually stole children away from their families. Kidnappings and forced conscriptions occur in other countries too. This boy was taken by an army in the Democratic Republic of Congo when he was 13:

❝ When they came to my village, they asked my older brother whether he was ready to join the militia. He was just 17 and he said no; they shot him in the head. Then they asked me if I was ready to sign, so what could I do – I didn't want to die. ❞

AFRICAN CHILD SOLDIERS

● It is estimated that Africa has over 120,000 child soldiers.

● African countries that use child soldiers include:
Algeria, Angola, Burundi, Chad, Congo, Democratic Republic of Congo, Eritrea, Ethiopia, Ivory Coast, Liberia, Rwanda, Sierra Leone, Somalia, Sudan and Uganda.

● The United Nations (UN) estimated that there were 20,000 or more child soldiers in Uganda's LRA from 2003 to 2005.

IS IT RIGHT TO FIGHT FOR RELIGION?

Religion has played a key role in many wars, from the First Crusade in the eleventh century to conflicts in the Middle East today. Christians, Muslims, Hindus and others have all battled violently for their faith. Can it ever be right to fight for religion?

Holy land?

Kashmir is a territory in South Asia that is split between India, Pakistan and China. Muslims in Pakistan and Hindus in India do not accept each other's claim on the land. They have fought several wars over the region, fuelled by religious differences. This Hindu extremist from Jammu, on the Indian side, is willing to fight to banish Muslims from Kashmir:

❝ Kashmir belongs to India. There are attacks on Hindus almost every day in Kashmir. Is it so wrong to retaliate? We want to make this land unsafe for Muslims to live in. Hindus must unite to expel Muslim [people] from the area. ❞

Muslim Kashmiri demonstrators throw stones at Indian riot police in Srinagar in August 2008.

> **"Religious wars are not caused by the fact that there is more than one religion, but by the spirit of intolerance..."**
> Charles de Secondat, French philosopher (1689–1755).

Hundreds of Muslim children march for peace in Manila, the Philippines in January 2008. In this country there has been conflict between Muslims and Christians for centuries.

What happened to tolerance?

Most religions preach tolerance of other faiths or beliefs. Many of their followers reject the violence used by those with more extreme religious views. Pieter De Vries, 15, from Staphorst in the Netherlands, believes that it would always be wrong to kill for your religion:

❝ War – no, it's wrong to fight for your religion. I do defend or fight for my beliefs, yes... but I would never kill for my religion. The only way forward is non-violence. It is much more difficult to turn the other cheek, but you are a stronger, better person for doing it. Martin Luther King and Gandhi were shining lights in the world... because they did not fight with force. ❞

IS NATIONAL SERVICE A GOOD IDEA?

In some countries, almost everyone has to spend some time in the armed forces. This is known as national service. Does it benefit a country and its people if most citizens are trained to fight in this way?

Waste of time

Many young conscripts do not enjoy the experience of national service. Laurent Chazal from Dijon, France served in the French army at the age of 18. He left just before compulsory national service was abolished in his country in 2001:

❝ For me personally, I thought it was a waste of time. They could have made better use of us, in a way. I mean there's great potential in a whole bunch of people together like that. If people do have to do national service in their country, I'd say do the civil service work instead. ❞

"I regard the principle of conscription of life [national service] as a flat contradiction of all our cherished ideals of individual freedom, democratic liberty and Christian teaching."

Roger Nash Baldwin, one of the founders of the American Civil Liberties Union (ACLU).

French conscripts train during part of their compulsory national service, before the system ended in 2001.

Valuable discipline

In Israel, most teenagers join the Defence Forces when they finish their high-school exams. Women join for 21 months, men for 36 months. Noa Katz completed her national service in 2007. Although she did not want to stay in the army, she thought her time spent in the forces was worthwhile:

" Many teenagers come out of school with very little idea of who they are or what they want to be in life. Doing national service in the military was a very good experience for me. I think I grew up, really. Everyone said I had a lot more confidence with people afterwards. I could mix with anyone, different social classes. And it's very good discipline. "

"Conscription [national service] is the vitality of a nation, the purification of its morality, and the real foundations of all its habits."

Napoleon I, French military and political leader (1769–1821).

NATIONAL SERVICE WORLDWIDE

Australia	none
China	selective conscription (2 years)
Israel	males 3 years, females 21 months
Italy	none (ended in 2005)
France	none (ended in 2001)
Germany	9 months
Norway	1 year (in practice shortened to 8 or 9 months)
Singapore	2 years–30 months (typical duration for all males)
United Kingdom	none (ended in 1963)
USA	none

IS EVACUATION A GOOD IDEA?

During a war, governments sometimes decide to send civilians, especially children, to the safety of the countryside or a neighbouring country. This is called evacuation. Is evacuation a good idea?

Great escape

When World War II began in 1939, millions of British children were evacuated to the countryside. They left their homes and families far behind in the city. Many young evacuees enjoyed the freedom of their time away. Jim Owen, aged 6 at the time of evacuation, found it exciting experiencing new things:

❝ It was a different world. I'd never been to a farm before. It was a dairy farm. We had sandwiches and milk to drink and I used to help Mr Dace cut the long grass in the fields. They used to milk the cows by hand. I'd never had fresh milk before – it was always condensed milk at home. It was like a holiday in the country. ❞

During World War II, three young evacuees from London discover the pleasures of country life at a Sussex farm.

Ethnic Albanian evacuees arrive by bus at Stankovic NATO camp in Macedonia, in April 1999.

Unsettling experience

Not everyone has a good experience of evacuation. Some people feel miserable, lost and frightened when they are sent miles away from home. In 1999, the United Nations began evacuating people from the war-torn Federal Republic of Yugoslavia. Filip, a Kosovo Albanian, was a child evacuee at the time. He was sent abroad, but never settled:

❝ We got met at the airport – lots of people asked us questions. Once we were through all that, my uncle and I went in a bus to a special centre... We had a house to stay in, but it wasn't like home. I had no idea where I was. I missed my friends like mad. I cried and I cried. My uncle kept saying, 'At least it's safe here.' I just wanted to go home. ❞

LEAVING KOSOVO

- By the end of May 1999, hundreds of thousands of Kosovans had been expelled from their homes.

- Most fled to neighbouring countries such as Albania and Macedonia.

- The overall number of people leaving Kosovo under the humanitarian evacuation programme was about 68,000 (less than a tenth of the total number of refugees).

- Countries accepting evacuees included the USA, Canada, Australia, the UK and many European nations.

IS WAR A WASTE OF MONEY?

Preparing for war is a costly exercise. Including all military expenses, the annual defence budget for the USA comes to over US$700 billion. Is this enormous military spending a waste of money, or is it worth the price?

Worth the price

Some people believe that you cannot put a price on protecting people. They say that when armies are fighting for a good or just cause, finance should not be an issue. Matt, a teenager from New Zealand, feels it is important to support the decisions of the military, no matter what the cost. He was in favour of the invasions of Iraq and Afghanistan:

❝ There are countries with a history of problems like Afghanistan and Iraq... Soldiers do well to stand up and risk their lives in combat. You get the cynics and anti-war lobby saying stop wasting taxpayers' money. But I think some things are worth fighting for. ❞

An aircraft hangar houses an array of expensive US missiles. Satellite-guided bombs like these cost thousands of dollars each.

Shameful costs

Other people argue that warfare is too expensive – that the money would be better used to feed hungry people or pay for medicines to help the sick. How can huge spending on arms be justified when millions of people around the world are dying of poverty? Some people suggest that wars are really fought for the benefit of richer nations anyway. Roger Davies, 17, from Bridgend in Wales, is one of them:

❝ War is such a shocking waste of resources. It is a waste of money and it's a waste of lives. The politicians only seem to be interested in one thing, and that's oil in the Middle East. How can you measure people's lives against oil or money? ❞

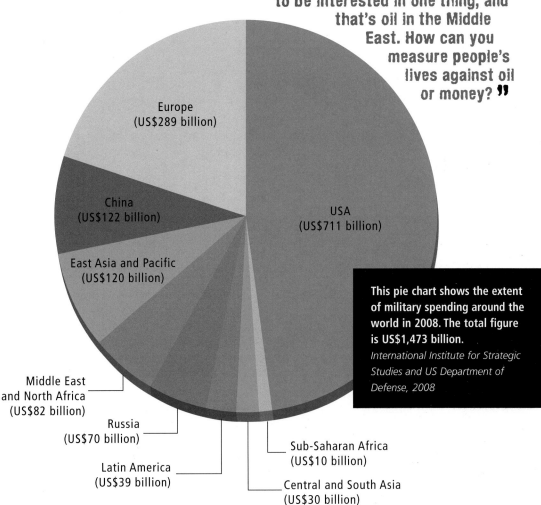

Europe (US$289 billion)

China (US$122 billion)

USA (US$711 billion)

East Asia and Pacific (US$120 billion)

Middle East and North Africa (US$82 billion)

Russia (US$70 billion)

Latin America (US$39 billion)

Sub-Saharan Africa (US$10 billion)

Central and South Asia (US$30 billion)

This pie chart shows the extent of military spending around the world in 2008. The total figure is US$1,473 billion.
International Institute for Strategic Studies and US Department of Defense, 2008

"At a time when we're on the brink of recession... ordinary Americans are paying a price for this war. When Iraq is costing each [US] household about 100 dollars a month you're paying a price for this war... by the time it's over this could be a 3 trillion dollar war."
Barack Obama, US president, 2008.

SHOULD WEAPONS OF MASS DESTRUCTION BE ALLOWED?

Weapons of Mass Destruction (WMDs) include nuclear, biological and chemical weapons. They can destroy huge numbers of civilians, on a scale that surpasses any other kind of warfare. Should WMDs be allowed to exist in the world?

Blasting an end to war

Some people argue that WMDs can save lives. In 1945, the world's first nuclear bombs destroyed the Japanese cities of Hiroshima and Nagasaki. This forced Japan to surrender and brought World War II to an end. Gregory Allen from Manhattan, USA, was 9 when the first atom bombs were used:

❝ We had to drop the bomb on Hiroshima... Japan surrendered and World War II was finally over. No one had tried dropping a nuclear bomb before. It was a terrible thing to do... but it definitely saved lives in the long run. ❞

It was probably true that fewer people died than would have been killed in an invasion of Japan. US President Truman had been advised that invading could lead to a million allied casualties alone.

This huge mushroom cloud rose above the Japanese city of Nagasaki after the nuclear bombing of 1945. This event effectively ended World War II.

HIROSHIMA AND NAGASAKI

The temperature at the centre of the Hiroshima and Nagasaki explosions reached 4,000 °C. The firestorms that followed the attack also claimed many lives:

● The bomb on Hiroshima directly killed roughly 70,000 people. Some estimates say that up to 200,000 victims had died by 1950, due to cancer or other effects of the chemicals.

● The Nagasaki bomb caused about 75,000 deaths.

"The chemical attack on Halabja, just one of 40 targeted at Iraq's own people, provided a glimpse of the crimes Saddam Hussein is willing to commit, and the kind of threat he now presents to the entire world. He is among history's cruellest dictators, and he is arming himself with the world's most terrible weapons."

George W Bush, 43rd US president, 2003 (prior to US invasion of Iraq).

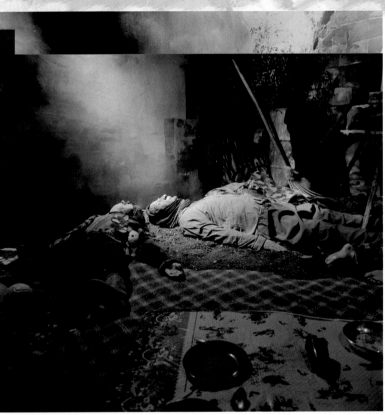

Halabja's Holocaust Museum in Iraq remembers the thousands of Kurdish victims who died during a poison gas attack in 1988.

Terrible effects

Many people believe that WMDs should never be allowed. There is widespread concern about the weapons getting into the wrong hands. In 1988, the Iraqi ruler Saddam Hussein used WMDs in his own country. He ordered a poison gas attack on the Kurdish town of Halabja, as a 'warning' to Kurdish people who opposed him. Roza Hamaseed, then aged 17, survived:

❝ Animals were running around in circles before they dropped down dead. Birds just fell out of the trees. There were these thick clouds of chemicals. And people screaming, covering their eyes. A lot of us were blinded by the gas, but just tried to run. Children dropped to the ground, fighting for their breath. You cannot imagine it... I don't know how many of us died... it was heartbreaking. ❞

CAN A COUNTRY RECOVER FROM WAR?

The way a war is fought, who wins, and the overall outcome all stick in people's minds long after the fighting is over. War also makes its mark on a country's landscape, economy and even reputation. Can this ever be put right?

Eritreans collect food supplies from a United Nations truck. After years of conflict, two-thirds of Eritrea's population still relies on foreign aid.

Economic ruin

The wreckage left by war can cripple a country's economy. Repairs to damaged buildings and infrastructure may involve huge expense, while individuals struggle to return to work and rebuild their own lives. Decades of fighting with Ethiopia (1963–1993) left the African nation of Eritrea relying heavily on foreign aid. President Isaias Afewerki commented:

❝ We have been left with a very shattered economy... The time everyone in this country will feel relieved will be when we are not asking anyone to give us any help. We would like to reach a stage where we can talk as equals to anyone, without asking for assistance or relief. ❞

Eritrea gained independence from the war, but it remains one of the poorest countries in the world.

The Old Town of Mostar in the south of Bosnia and Herzegovina is recovering from the Bosnian War. More than half a million tourists visited the city in 2007.

Living with the past

War can also leave survivors with severe emotional scars. Few people in Bosnia will forget the ruthless 'ethnic cleansing' by Serb and Croat forces in 1992–1995. But many Bosnians also see a need to move on. Fadila, a Bosnian Muslim, lost her son in Srebrenica in 1995. Ten years later, she said:

❝ I don't have a future. I only have a past. But I still think the town has a future, maybe in 70 years... The mine, the factory, the woods and tourism. We still have all of that. But it needs to be repaired. ❞

Mirad was just a child when Croatian soldiers banished his family at gunpoint from their home. Now he studies at a mainly Croat university:

❝ We've built some bridges between us. We're not thinking about the war and for us that's great. I have lots of Croatian friends and we go out together. The future I think will be better for our generation. ❞

BOSNIAN LOSSES

- Around 100,000 soldiers and civilians were killed in the Bosnia-Herzegovina war.
- An estimated 2.2 million people (more than half of the country's population) were forced from their homes.
- Around 0.5 million refugees have never returned.

IS WAR THE LAST RESORT?

War is a desperate measure. A country's decision to wage war with another nation is never taken lightly. But at what point do a country's rulers decide that the talking has to stop, and that war is a necessity?

Talk first

Many people feel that every possible way of avoiding war should always be explored before the fighting starts. Sometimes arguments between rival groups or countries can be solved through talks. Sanctions (trade and economic punishments) may persuade a country to change its behaviour. Hanif El-Attar, 16, from Cairo, Egypt, reasons:

❝ A country should try everything else first before going to war. You can put pressure on another country, by withdrawing aid or using UN sanctions. And peace is always possible... look at Sudan. The Sudanese government and the southern rebels finally made peace in 2005 [after nearly 50 years of war]. Why can't they do the same in Darfur? ❞

The United Nations Security Council holds meetings to discuss peace and impose sanctions, to try to prevent conflict around the world.

"We recognise that self-defence is always the primary reason for war, and even then can be only a last resort. Unless you've exhausted everything else, it's very hard to justify [war]."
Dr Rowan Williams, 104th Archbishop of Canterbury, United Kingdom, 2003.

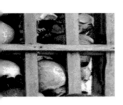

"Throughout history, it has been the inaction of those who could have acted; the indifference of those who should have known better; the silence of the voice of justice when it mattered most; that has made it possible for evil to triumph."

Haile Selassie, Emperor of Ethiopia (1930–1974).

An estimated 1.5 million Cambodians died under the 1975–1979 Khmer Rouge regime, led by the dictator Pol Pot. A Cambodian boy looks at the remains of some of the victims at a memorial.

Action speaks louder

Some people feel that after a certain point, to talk for longer just gives the enemy more time to prepare for war. They suggest that more lives are saved in the long-run if decisive action is taken against threatening regimes. Julie Stirling, 18, is a student of modern history in Edinburgh, Scotland:

❝ People talk about... [war being used as a] 'last resort', but sometimes you shouldn't wait too long to act. You have to act rather than turn a blind eye, pretending it's not happening. We waited too long to stop Adolf Hitler, Pol Pot [in Cambodia] and Saddam Hussein. We should have the courage of our convictions... and get rid of evil leaders like that... sooner rather than later. ❞

WHAT IS THE FUTURE OF WAR?

Throughout history, conflict seems to have been a fact of life. There may be ways to resolve disputes and tensions without fighting. But can we hope for a more peaceful future – or will people always wage war?

Hope for peace

Since the end of World War II, the Middle East has been one of the most conflict-ridden parts of the world. Today, wars and armed disputes are still regular events. Even so, Hila Weill, a 14-year-old Israeli, thinks that peace could one day come to the region:

❝ For every terrible act of war, there is someone else doing something good. We do not want war with our Arab neighbours... Peace and co-operation may seem a long way off, but it is the only way. ❞

An Israeli child and his Palestinian friend hope for a peaceful future.

"Mankind must put an end to war, or war will put an end to mankind."
John F Kennedy, 35th US president (1961–1963).

"It is easier to lead men to combat, stirring up their passion, than to restrain them and direct them toward the patient labours of peace."
André Gide, French author (1869–1951).

This woman and child from southern Darfur have returned to their home, destroyed by Janjaweed militants in 2004. Their future remains bleak.

WAR IN DARFUR

- Since 2003, 200,000 people have been killed in the Darfur conflict.

- 2 million Darfurians have fled to refugee camps in Sudan.

- Up to 250,000 have fled to neighbouring Chad.

Fighting for ever

Some people feel that human nature does not change and that war will never end. Conflicts continue to happen all around the world, even though people are aware of the consequences. Fatma, 17, lives in war-torn Darfur, Sudan. She cannot understand how humans can act so barbarically to one another, but she has so far survived the experience. For her, this is how the world works:

They came at night and fired their guns at villagers. You might ask how the Janjaweed could do this... shooting women and children... burning and looting our village... But it is the same story all over our country. Now we have nothing. We have lost our families, our friends. Kill someone and your own humanity dies too. But war goes on.

TIMELINE

475–221 BC Warring States Era in China. Regional warlords take over nearby smaller states in China.

AD 1095–1099 The First Crusade. The first of many military campaigns is waged by Christians from Europe against Muslims in the Middle East.

13th century Mongol Conquests. Genghis Khan conquers vast territories across China, Central Asia, Persia and into Europe.

1455–1458 Wars of the Roses. Civil wars are fought in England between the Houses of York and Lancaster.

1618–1648 Thirty Years' War. This religious war in Germany starts between Protestants and Catholics, but ends up being a political war involving most of Europe.

1642–1651 English Civil War – a series of armed conflicts between Parliamentarians and Royalists.

1804–1815 Napoleonic Wars. Napoleon's French Empire extends until 1812, when the invasion of Russia ends disastrously for Napoleon.

1851–1864 Taiping Rebellion. A large-scale revolt against the authority of the Qing government in China ends in a death toll of up to 30 million people.

1861–1865 American Civil War. Civil war rages between southern slave states and the US federal government, or the 'Union'. Union victory strengthens the role of the government.

1914–1918 World War I. A huge war takes place mainly in Europe after the assassination of Archduke Franz Ferdinand, heir to the Austro-Hungarian throne.

1929 to present Conflict between Arabs and Jewish settlers. After Israel is formed in 1948, this ongoing conflict includes several wars, including the 1948 Arab-Israeli War and the Six-Day War of 1967. In December 2008 Israel attacks the Palestinian territory of Gaza, and over a thousand Palestinians are killed, before a ceasefire at the end of January 2009.

1939–1945 World War II. Global conflict mobilises over 100 million troops, with a death toll of about 70 million people. Two superpowers emerge – the Soviet Union and the USA. Cold War between the two powers follows for the next 45 years.

1950–1953 Korean War. This border war between North and South Korea ends up involving Russia and the USA, fighting for the north and the south, respectively.

1954–1975 Vietnam War. This is fought between the communist North Vietnam, supported by communist allies, and South Vietnam. From 1965, the USA fights in support of the South. North Vietnam captures the capital Saigon in 1975, and the country is reunified in 1976.

1980–1988 Iran-Iraq War. Iraq uses chemical weapons, such as mustard gas, against Iranians, as well as against Iraqi Kurds.

1983–2005 Second Sudanese Civil War. This civil war between the country's north and south continues where a previous one (1955–1972) left off.

1988 to present Somali Civil War. Armed conflict in this unstable country is characterised by inter-clan fighting between competing warlords.

1990–1994 Rwandan Civil War. Ethnic tensions flare up into the infamous Rwandan Genocide, as the Hutu majority massacres the Tutsi minority and Hutu moderates.

1991 The First Gulf War. Coalition forces, led chiefly by the USA and UK, defeat Iraq after Saddam Hussein's invasion of Kuwait.

1992–1995 Bosnian War. War in Bosnia and Herzegovina involves many factions (groups) and crimes against humanity, the worst being the massacre of Bosnian Muslims in Srebrenica.

1996–1999 Kosovo War. Serbian and Yugoslav security forces fight the Kosovo Liberation Army (seeking separation from the former Yugoslavia). In 1999, NATO attacks Yugoslav targets and Kosovo Albanian refugees pour into neighbouring countries.

2001–2002 US invasion of Afghanistan. The beginning of George W Bush's 'War on Terror'. The aim is to capture Osama bin Laden and to remove the Taliban regime. Bin Laden remains at large.

2003 to present Darfur conflict, western Sudan. This dispute is tribal and ethnic rather than religious. The Sudanese government and the Janjaweed militia carry out attacks on villages in Darfur, leading to the mass departure of refugees.

2003 to present Iraq War. This ongoing conflict (or military occupation) begins with the US-led invasion of Iraq to depose Iraqi dictator Saddam Hussein. A new democratic government is established, but civil strife continues within the country, particularly between Sunni and Shi'ite Muslims.

2008 South Ossetia War. War between Russia and Georgia takes place over the independence of the region of South Ossetia.

GLOSSARY

anaesthetic A substance used to take away the feeling of pain, for example, during an operation.

atom bomb A nuclear bomb – a type of Weapon of Mass Destruction (WMD).

civilian A person who is not a member of the armed forces or the police.

civil war War between different groups in the same country.

communist Related to communism, a political and economic system that claims to put the interests of society as a whole above those of the individual.

conflict A dispute, struggle or war between opposing sides.

conscription Compulsory enrolment into military service.

democracy A political system in which the people elect their own leaders.

economy The goods, services and wealth produced by a society.

ethnic cleansing The elimination of a particular group of people from a society or region.

ethnic group A group sharing the same race, culture and/or language.

evacuation Removing people to a safer area during a war or other disaster.

foreign aid The help, such as economic assistance, offered by one nation to another.

front line The centre of combat in a conflict or war.

genocide Deliberately killing a nationality or particular group of people.

guerrilla A member of an irregular armed force.

infrastructure The basic facilities and services that help a society to work well. This usually includes transport, factories, schools and water and power lines.

Janjaweed Armed groups of men fighting on the side of the government in Darfur, western Sudan.

martyr A person willing to lose his or her life rather than give up religious faith.

massacre The savage killing of large numbers of people, often in battle.

militia A body of unofficial, not professional, soldiers.

NATO North Atlantic Treaty Organisation – a grouping of 26 nations that have agreed to join together in defence against external attack.

occupation (military) When one nation invades the territory of another nation, with the intention of holding it, even temporarily.

pacifist A person who believes that violence, including war, is always wrong.

refugees People who have been forced to leave their homes (usually crossing a border to find safety in a neighbouring country).

resources Goods, raw materials, money and services used by people to achieve a goal.

sanctions Special restrictions or penalties threatened or carried out as a punishment.

United Nations (UN) An international organisation with over 190 member countries, which was formed in 1945 to promote world peace, good health and economic development.

RESOURCES

Books

On the Front Line: In the Trenches in World War I (Freestyle Express) by Adam Hibbert (Raintree, 2006)

World War II (Eyewitness) by Simon Adams and Andy Crawford (Dorling Kindersley, 2004)

Sudan (Global Hotspots) by Geoff Barker (Macmillan Library, 2008)

Dictatorship (Systems of Government) by Paul Dowswell (Evans Brothers, 2005)

Religious Extremism (Voices) by Otto James (Evans Brothers, 2006)

DVDs

Children of War: The Evacuees (Artsmagic, 2007)
This documentary tells the story of children evacuated to the countryside during World War II.

Iraq in Fragments by James Longley (Drakes Avenue Pictures, 2007) Classification 12.
This documentary shows life carrying on in occupied Iraq – seen through the eyes of three children with different ethnic backgrounds.

The World at War TV series narrated by Laurence Olivier (Fremantle Home Entertainment, 2005)
The definitive documentary about World War II focuses on key themes – from the rise of Nazi Germany to the beginning of the Cold War between the former Soviet Union and the USA.

Websites

http://www.bbc.co.uk/history/trail/wars_conflict
This website has a selection of audio and visual clips, quizzes and activities on many different war subjects.

http://www.bbc.co.uk/worldservice/specials/1624_story_of_africa
Many African countries have been at war in recent years. Find out the story of Africa from its earliest days.

http://www.unicef.org/emerg
The United Nations website has lots of up-to-date information on current emergencies, including work carried out by UNICEF (United Nations Children's Emergency Fund) in many war-torn countries. Includes a 'Voices of Youth' section.

http://www.unhcr.org
This website for the United Nations refugee agency provides information about refugees all over the world, most of them displaced by warfare.

http://www.warchild.org
This website focuses on the children trapped in wars and conflicts throughout the world.

INDEX